FR

D1263441

READING POWER

> **Helping Organizations** <

The Peace Corps

Anastasia Suen

The Rosen Publishing Group's

PowerKids Press™
New York

Published in 2002 by The Rosen Publishing Group, Inc.
29 East 21st Street, New York, NY 10010

First Edition

Book Design: Michelle Innes

Photo Credits: © The Peace Corps

Suen, Anastasia.
The Peace Corps / by Anastasia Suen.
   p. cm. — (Helping organizations)
Includes bibliographical references and index.
ISBN 0-8239-6001-3
1. Peace Corps (U.S.)—Juvenile literature. [1. Peace Corps (U.S.)]
I. Title.
HC60.5 .S88 2002
361.6—dc21

                              2001000603

Manufactured in the United States of America

Contents

The Peace Corps Begins

John F. Kennedy was the president of the United States from 1961 to 1963. He wanted Americans to help people in other countries. He wanted peace around the world. John F. Kennedy started the Peace Corps on March 1, 1961.

John F. Kennedy spoke about forming a Peace Corps before he became president.

Governments of other countries ask for help from the Peace Corps. The Peace Corps sends people to help countries in need.

It's a Fact

Since 1961, the Peace Corps has helped 134 countries!

7

Volunteers

The people who work in the
Peace Corps are volunteers.
Volunteers do not get paid
for their work.

It's a Fact

Over 161,000 people have volunteered for the Peace Corps.

The volunteers work with the Peace Corps for two years. The Peace Corps teaches them how to help before they can work.

It's a Fact

Peace Corps volunteers
have to train for three months
before they can work. Some
volunteers have to learn a
new language.

Helping Others

Peace Corps volunteers help hundreds of thousands of people each year. The Peace Corps helps people help themselves.

Volunteers Help in Many Ways

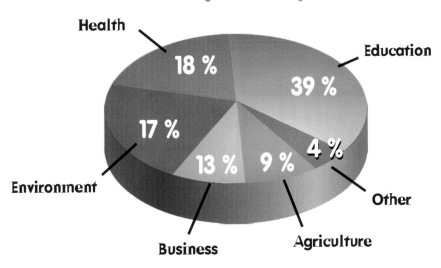

Health
18 %

Education
39 %

17 %

13 %

9 %

4 %

Environment

Business

Agriculture

Other

Volunteers help remove a beehive from some bushes in Ghana in Africa.

Volunteers teach many new skills to people all over the world. Some volunteers help teach children. Volunteers also help to build schools and other buildings.

Peace Corps volunteers help build a new school in Gabon in Africa.

15

Some countries need help with farming. Volunteers help people find new ways to grow food. Other countries need doctors or nurses. Volunteers help where they are needed.

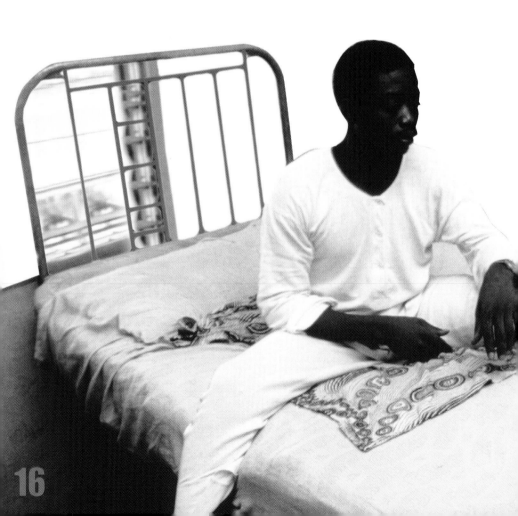

Volunteering in the Peace Corps is hard work, but it can also be fun. Volunteers meet many new people and see many different places.

 Peace Corps volunteers play a game of touch football with children in their village.

The Peace Corps Today

Today, more than 7,000 Peace Corps volunteers are at work in 76 countries all over the world. People are able to live healthier and happier lives with the help of the Peace Corps.

The Peace Corps at Work

21

Glossary

corps (**kor**) a group of people with specialized training

governments (**guv**-uhrn-muhnts) groups of people who rule or manage countries

language (**lang**-gwij) the speech of one nation or other large group of people

peace (**peas**) freedom from war

volunteers (vahl-uhn-**teers**) people who work without pay

Resources

Books

So, You Want to Join the Peace Corps: What to Know Before You Go
by Dillon Banerjee
Ten Speed Press (1999)

The Kid's Guide to Service Projects: Over 500 Service Ideas for Young People Who Want to Make a Difference
by Barbara A. Lewis
Free Spirit Publishing, Inc. (1995)

Web Site
http://www.peacecorps.gov/kids/index.html

Index

Word Count: 268

Note to Librarians, Teachers, and Parents

If reading is a challenge, Reading Power is a solution! Reading Power is perfect for readers who want high-interest subject matter at an accessible reading level. These fact-filled, photo-illustrated books are designed for readers who want straightforward vocabulary, engaging topics, and a manageable reading experience. With clear picture/text correspondence, leveled Reading Power books put the reader in charge. Now readers have the power to get the information they want and the skills they need in a user-friendly format.